COCO WAYS

Coco Ways

A Tribute To African American Women

Selected Poems by
Darren Reed

AYA PUBLISHING YORKTOWN, VIRGINIA

AYA PUBLISHING

AYA Publishing
5007 C Victory Blvd.
Suite # 191
Yorktown, Virginia 23693

Copyright © 1999 by Darren Reed

ISBN 0-9670325-0-4

Book Design by: AYA Publishing
Cover Photos taken from the Reed and Hill
family collections.

Manufactured in the United States of America

This book is dedicated to my wife
Courtney, my mother Jacqueline
and African American women
everywhere.

Acknowledgments

First of all, I give thanks and praise to the Creator for all opportunities, successes, and failures. To me, they are all blessings.

I would like to thank my wife Courtney (Coco), whose "Coco Ways" make for easy writing. I could not have completed this book without her patience, inspiration, and editing.

I would also like to thank Mandral Blackmon and Quammie Newsome who offered motivation and suggestions. Their individual talents and energy have been motivating factors in the completion of this book.

I am indebted to Barbara Dudley, an experienced and talented writer who helped me appreciate many aspects of writing and publishing.

Lastly, I extend love and thanks to my entire family, Mom, Dad, Deon, Devin, Danielle, Dominique, as well as the Hills, my other family. Thank You.

Contents

-Contents-

-Contents-

BROTHERS GONNA WORK IT OUT

PAUL HILL, JR.

Foreword

Coco Ways represents a refreshing collection of poems by Darren Reed. This volume of poems was written to pay tribute to the African American woman. The poems in this book depict personal experiences that touch the heart, mind, and soul of the readers.

Coco Ways is dedicated to the author's wife, affectionately known as "Coco." Darren and Coco complement each other as soul mates. The foundation of *Coco Ways* is predicated on the author's healthy relationship with African American women in his life. This volume of poetry represents a celebration of those relationships and serves as a wake-up· call for brothers that says "sorry" is not enough!

The first section of *Coco Ways* contains poems that celebrate the African American woman for her courage, strength, perseverance, love and beauty. The second section of the book speaks to the urgency of African

-Foreword-

American men establishing and nurturing relationships with African American women that are predicated on respect, honesty, trust, and sharing.

Darren Reed is to be commended for this collection of poems that represents a variety of styles from romance to rap that celebrates the African American woman.

-Paul Hill, Jr.
Author-Cleveland, Ohio

Preface

I wasn't surprised to see African American women as a recurring theme in my writing. Poetry can be therapeutic, offering writers an avenue to express eloquently what they otherwise may never confront. *Coco Ways* is a collection of poems about the African American women who have played major roles in my development as a man and as a person. Whether marveling at their strength and courage or basking in their beauty, I have developed an appreciation for the African American women in my life. These poems are a reflection of my sentiments for our sisters.

African American women often face a double-edged sword in a society that struggles with equality for all citizens. Not only are they subjected to the ills of racism, they also struggle with the inequities that women in general, face in a male dominated society.

Despite this often difficult reality, African American women have, and continue to, display great resiliency and character as they

-Preface-

struggle to maintain the essence, culture, and strength of African American families and communities.

These poems reflect my personal experiences as well as the experiences of other African American men. I have found that many brothers share these same sentiments, but for a variety of reason, fail to communicate those feelings.

The last section of the book contains poems about us brothers, the seemingly missing link from the chains of our families and communities. These poems depict some of our experiences and speak to the urgency of African American men joining our women in the effort to catapult our communities to farther, more positive heights.

-Darren Reed
Newport News, Virginia 1999

COCO WAYS

Love

Courage

Strength

Perseverance

Empty Rocker
(For Ms. Bolden)

She rocked bundled kids
to school each morning
sipping from a plastic
cup filled with love.
The number of her rocks are
in the thousands,
rocking generations on.

She was the neighborhood watch,
commanding respect with each rock,
offering warm hugs *and*
switch whippings.

She met dawn in the rocker
and rocked the stars to our block
at night. A baby sitter to
my mom *and* me, an institution.

Her rocker is empty now
and nearby kids run wild.
My children won't know the joy
and comfort of her rocking,
my stories will have to do.

The Natural

Rare like South African gems
From her hair to her soul is pure
A pleasant breeze on a hot summer's day
She's a natural sistah for sure
No make-up to make up her face
A natural wonder in a made up place

Built like mountains curved and strong
Feet planted firmly on the ground
Her locks are short but her roots run long
A natural resource in her I've found
No make-up to make up her face
A natural sistah in this made up place

It Ain't Just You

According to them,
the numbers begin and end with you.
A sea of sisters feeding
this welfare beast.

According to them,
you endure the pain of
childbirth for more
books of colored money
and cheap rent-
even you sister, struggling
to stack brown ones and purple fives
to feed your seeds and save lives.

According to them,
the beast is black,
an amalgamation of baby-toting
sisters living with their
hands out for extra handouts.

But you and I know
the data is falsified, misleading
like the eleven o'clock news.

The lighter side of the beast
is overlooked.
But you and I both know,
it ain't just you.

We're Together

You sing Oliver musical tunes
I prefer the Stylistics
but we're together

You cherish the silence of the country
while I search for peace in the city
but we're still together

I like 103 JAMZ
You'd rather listen to the BBC
but we're still together

You pay things in advance
I'd rather send "minimum due"
but we're still together

You love me and I love you
I guess that's why we're still together

Her

To **her** they're just feet
plain and necessary, dressed up
by 9 Wests
and mocha brown
nail polish
dangling exposed in the air
suspended by curved, crossed legs.
To me they're more,
making chill bumps rise on my skin.
I'm lost in **her** scent, caught up by
each move she makes;
her breathing, **her** sighs,
the movement of **her** thighs,
the blinking of **her** eyes.
I'm lost in **her** back, long and lean
and the way it's just there
unseen by **her**.
I hug **her**, inhaling **her** scent
but she wiggles to escape
(I just hugged **her** minutes ago)
My eyes know **her** beauty
inside and out.
I smile because of **her**.

Strugglin'

Mama, whether you believe it or not
what you heard is true
I'm giving the world all I got
just like you told me to

But when I reach open doors
they soon close tight
they see my face and all in haste
smiling faces grow fright

I've been honest like you said
and learned all the three R's
where we live is confusing, Mama
and inside I'm left with scars

What's that? Keep my head high?
Mama, you know that I will
you taught me how to struggle on
even if it's all uphill

Honduran Summer

Caribbean breezes stroll gently
along her face, hugging
the contours of her beauty.
White sands mold her,
leaving imprints of hearts turned
upside down along the shore.
Echoes of my thoughts beckon to her
but she doesn't hear.
Through squinting eyes I peer,
watching the sun kiss apricot hues
across her body, matching
her with the glowing sunset.
I followed her to this paradise
where she and its purity are one.
I snap mental pictures
hoping to still-frame her essence
but it is too free to capture.
Inhaling the summertime air,
pleasure consumes me.
I asked her to marry me today,
she said yes.

Four in the Morning

Head hung low, she speaks
through a sunkened heart.
Between the smoke clouds I see her,
a true woman. Her frame
maintained well after five kids.
I notice her triceps, taking me
back to younger days when
hours found me squeezing them in
some juvenile attempt at security.
Decades from then I sit, wanting
to embrace her pain and rock
her to sleep. But her pride wouldn't
allow me to forget who the Mama is.
Instead I sit back and love her
and cry all at once.
Her eyes speak of dreams differed
and fallen stars, but they don't
shed tears. I know they're there,
symbolically pouring down the
outside of the glass clutched
in once pearl smooth hands.
Do I tell her it's going to
be all right, or do I kiss my mama
good night?

Coco Ways

They belong to her , like
stars to an Alabama night.
Simple yet complex,
subtle, yet obvious to me.
I know them better than my own.
They come and go like tides,
like changing seasons.
I ride them until the next
one comes along.
Strong, yet gentle,
relaxed, yet charged.
They belong to her, like
stars to an Alabama night,
and she shares them with me.

Thank You

Hair still like wool
fashioned as much as
tough roots allow.
Unjazzercized hips and thighs
you laugh at 1's and 2's
preferring to keep
your larger, natural size
Thank You.

Skin smooth,
made-up only by
the sun
you prefer your looks natural
unlike the other ones

You look past
my modest cash flow
into the soul of a brother,
different than the others
and I thank you.

Already

I looked forward to your trip,
unable to recall the last
time I was alone for days.
On the way to the airport
I listened casually while
you explained details of your trip.
Yet when I left the parking lot
for home and found you
were gone, I realized
I missed you already.

That's My Mama!

Have you ever met a woman
who can make miracle meals
with baking soda and bare cupboards?
That's my Mama!

You ever met a woman
whose looks can stop both men
and misbehaving kids dead in their tracks?
That's my Mama!

Do you know a woman
so proud of her kids that she
talks about them to anyone who
will listen?
That's my Mama!

Have you ever met a woman
who gets a phone call at work
about her child's behavior
and the next day there's
a new child at school?
That's my Mama!

Have you ever met a woman
who is a good mother to her
children and all the neighborhood
kids love her too?
That's my Mama!

Do you know a woman
whose children adore her
so much that they try all they
can to show her how much she's
loved, even writing poems about her?
That's my Mama!

Some Brothers

Some brothers search a lifetime
trying to find what I found,
a fine sistah feet firmly
on the ground
not caught up
in material things-
cars, diamond rings
(well, maybe diamonds)
I'm blessed in many ways
and count you as a
blessing each day

Some brothers pass you by
because they can tell in your eyes
you're not flattered by fast talking guys
or preoccupied with looking "fly"

Some brothers think it's
too much
to value a sistah' with
high standards and such
But the rewards are priceless,
you can be as warm as the sun
or as cold as ice is,

it just depends
on some brothers

Sistah

Like a palm tree she sways, hustling
through her days, moving to the sound
of her own melody,
unaware of what she does to me.
She is poetry- gliding with the assurance of
Angelou, the elegance of Hughes,
the beauty of words when
perfectly used. Her beauty flows
like perfect prose, all the brothers know,
but they only see, I feel her because
she's inside of me.
Smooth like a poets rhymes, off-beat
and on time, you should hear her sometimes,
she's so fine. Like Dunbar's written pieces,
I'm left speechless,
as her smile releases thoughts of boyhood
love crushes, love rushes through me, do me
baby, she drives me crazy, my vision get
hazy. I get chill bumps, a hot flash,
I want to grab her *assk* her questions.
Like shade from the Baobab tree, this sistah
comforts me. And when I close my eyes

she's mine like she's supposed to be.
Until I have her, I'll sit and stare,
at all the beautiful things around me,
because she is there.

Ceiba Night

We reached the rooftop
at Hotel Puerto Rico by candlelight.
The city was black, asleep.
I looked forward to this each day
as the natives conserve energy
during rainy season.
We overlooked the blackened
paradise and heard the city
breathe in its slumber.
Under moonlight we talked
of love and tomorrows deep
into the mahogany night,
until our candlelight
was extinguished by the morning sun.

When I Come Home

Mama tells everybody
when I come home,
even when I want to relax.
But she doesn't
have me but for so long each year
so I pick her up from work
and meet the strangers
who know me from
exaggerated stories and half truths.

When I come home I don't
sleep much, Mama keeps me
up and tells stories I've heard
before, each time with a
different ending.
But she doesn't have me but for
so long each year,
so I stay up and listen
and smile and return
to where I live exhausted.

When I come home Mama
doesn't have to catch
the city bus because

I'm home and I can take her
and she smiles, making
me pull up to the front where
everyone can see.

When I come home who
I am is simple, a part
of something that is
all of me. Mama pulls
out old pictures that seem
new each time I see them.
But she only has me but for so
long each year so I stay up
and laugh and reminisce until I fall
asleep on the good couch.
Mama usually yells for people not
to sit on the couch to keep it
clean, but she lets me, because she
only has me but for so long
each year.

In My Dream

In my dream she held me close,
told me I was the one
she needed the most. She
caressed my pain to the sound
of falling rain, her heart spoke my name.

In my dream I
squeezed her back,
held her closer and she liked that.
In love, we soar above,
weightless I was.

In my dream she was right here,
in my arms, in my love,
and all was clear.
I grinned as she pinched my skin,
praying she wouldn't pinch
me again. Nothing changed
it seemed. At that moment I
realized I was awake and she
was my dream.

Was it me?

Our eyes met in the crowded room and
danced in the smoky air, playing peek-a-boo
like infants. Our vibes mingled like old
friends and our scents escaped us, joining
each other, sharing sweetness
...or was it me?

All else disappeared, leaving the world to us
and we were alone in the room
...or was it me?

She pretended to bat lint from her eyes so
no one would notice I was the destination of
her batting eyes. And from across the room
I saw her laugh at humorless jokes just to
show me how beautiful her teeth were.
She strutted to the ladies' room so I could
see the strut of her caramel smooth legs
...or was it me?

She wrapped her lips, wet and full around
her straw, sucking slowly to show me she
liked to take things slow. She arched her

back in exaggeration, ran her fingers through
her hair, and turned sideways so I could see
her profile
...or was it me?

I swallowed my heart, pounding like a fist,
when she walked my way like a lioness
seeking prey. I closed my eyes and smiled,
my senses hadn't failed me. But when I
opened them she was gone. I turned only to
find that her playful night games led her to
the arms of another
...Damn, it was me.

Destiny

"Yo! Rewind that tape!
yeah, that's her,
the one I'm going to marry one day."

Those were my words
ten years ago,
we've been married for some time now
and still got forever to go

It's a cute story to tell,
one that's hard to believe
but things work out like that sometimes
when you believe in destiny.

I Get it From You

At times my
thoughts attack my tongue
and force themselves out
regardless of who's around.
And when the world tells me no
I smile inside knowing only
I can hold me down
I get it from you.

I have a tendency to look
for the good in others
despite what they do or say and
I get excited easily living life
as if each day is my last day
I get that from you.

A never-say-die spirit
regardless of what life brings,
I don't hesitate to call a spade
a spade and a host of other things.
I get it from you.

High cheek bones
blue skin and a desire to improve,

learning the rules of the games
and never playing to lose
Mama, I get it from you.

Sistah Soldia

She comes from a long
line of them,
strong sistahs all shades
of Africa! She knows
here purpose like Harriet
knew hers, always leading.
Each generation her tools for
revolution are traded in
for more effective ones.
Today she does it all
with laptops and
minivans and business suits-
complete with families and careers;
fearless, undying strength,
juggling all that she must
to carry on who she is
and what we need to become.

Forever

I greet the morning with her
sweetness on my lips, the
warmth of her hips, and soft
caresses of her fingertips.
She rocks my world
like slave ships. I
tighten my grip when
the night waves hit.
We sail into bliss, I never
felt like this.
The taste of her kiss is
something I'll never miss,
for she is the one
forever is with.

Swing Young Sister!
(For Venus Williams)

Swing young sister!
Zip the air for us all.
Breaking barriers with beads
and back-hands in territory
chartered only by a few who
look like you.

Swing young sister!
Represent those hidden treasures
in Compton and Cleveland
and Harlem and all over.
Show the world it can
be done anywhere,
even on green rectangles
where we're hard too find.

Swing young sister!
The ball is in you court!
Place it where you
want, we'll make sure
the call is right.

Inspiration to all of us,
showing what we can do
when the opportunities come
and we're prepared.
Swing young sister!

Christmas Without Mama

Donny Hathaway's "This Christmas"
is a blues song on the stereo now.
We slept late and crawled
out of bed like unenthused
kids at an opera.
Silence invades the house
and the crumpling of
presents from the kids
next door is loud.
We reluctantly shake boxes
she wrapped
the night before and
the snow we prayed for is
just white stuff outside now.
It's not the same without her.
My brother wears an expression
that says what I feel.
Nobody's Mama should have
to work on Christmas.

Candy Girl

I'm hooked
got a sweet tooth
like the candy I craved
in youth. Your flavors
are mine to savor
like cotton candy and
now & laters.
I'm sweet on your lips
and hips like chocolate
chips and fun dip.
In your eyes are brown
moon pies
and the sugar
has me high from
your tootsie roll thighs
smooth like honey.
Damn I need money
to buy a bag full of
you to unwrap and smack
the whole night through.

Time for You

You have known him, love
without knowing yourself
You have felt his pain
forgetting to embrace your own
You have lived his ways, love
unaware of your own style
You have danced his dance
ignoring your own music
You have given of yourself
unaware of what you deserve
You have traveled his road, love
unaware of your own path
You have yearned for his love
pushing aside love of self
You have caressed his pain
without soothing your own hurt
You have laughed at his jokes, love
ignoring your own wit...
this has to quit
It's time for you, love
It's time for you

Happy

Nothing is happening
that can be seen, but it's there.
She sits beside me, eyes fixed
on barren stretches of road,
her gentle hands gripping
the wheel. Summer air whips
through an open sunroof,
barley moving the curls
in her "natural."
Earth Wind and Fire croon to us,
providing theme music
for a wonderful life.
("Hearts of fire, creates love desire,
take you higher and higher...")
Tomorrow is not promised,
but today, I'm happy.

Livin' Large

We scurry to dismantle
towers of sticky jelly crackers,
effusing cloudy glasses of
sugar-water down
and often unused disposal.
With soapless rags and vigor
we wipe away remnants of our
distorted hunger,
scouring molars with
timeless baking soda
in the back of a hallow
fridge, ridding them of the
horror they faced. All this
because Mama just
pulled up with groceries
led by Captain Crunch
himself and,
at least for a while,
we shall live large.

Fifth Ward Blues

She stood before me in all
her splendor, chocolate and right.
Her ways were familiar to me.
I knew her though we just met—
maybe in a dream or a trip to
the Fifth Ward, who knows?
I touched her with extended arms
but the pleasure was also my pain.
She felt like mine and my skin
begged to be near hers, but our
eyes knew other loves.
We held on for dear life,
knowing time would soon take
us under. And time did come
that sunny afternoon.
My lips parted, forcing a reluctant
smile and farewell
Damn, a day late and a dollar
short. I'm holding on.

The Morning After
(Domestic Violence)

His dirty wine permeates
the morning air.
I prayed it was a
dream cruel and ugly, but
bitter reality illuminates
in broken glass on the floor.
Violent images sit clear in my mind
and my ears still ring
from the after-midnight
sound waves, high in decibels,
now light years in space.
I stand too weak for school,
had duty all night,
protecting you from him.
No class could teach what I
know anyway. My smile
will be extra wide today for
there is much to hide in
my soul. You finally made it
to sleep. I pray you're
dreaming of better days.

First Kiss

I barely knew myself, not to mention you
we sat on that bench all night
The barefoot running man distracted us
but that first kiss turned out right

Since then our lips have met
thousands of times I guess
but the joy of that awkward first kiss
will always outshine the rest

At Home in Winter

The cold of winter sneaks
in beneath a cool autumn
and in that instant things change.
Frosted glass separates us from
nor-easters and frost and
winds from the lake.
Sounds of crunching snow
and whistles of cold
bring us closer.
We enjoy our confinement,
unmatched by any
warm-front or Christmas
in shorts. A part of peace
is being home with you
in winter.

In Love

We kneel together behind
the Buick parked by the curb
hoping to go unseen by the hide-n-seek
Counter. A purple sun ducks
behind the city, giving way
to the glow of her
lightening-bug earrings.
I feel the softness of her hand
brush my arm as she balances herself,
nearly falling over from uncontrollable
giggles. A drop of cool has been
added to the night air
sending forth luke- warm breezes,
but they are no match for the goose bumps
on my skin. The game has ended and our
mothers have become the seekers. We
remain a few moments more, holding
fast to a feeling we can't describe.
I'm in love with two things,
summertime in the city
and the girl next door.

Good Morning, America
(For Harriet Tubman and others)

The night was long,
four hundred years-plus long,
they prayed dawn would
greet me.

Bodies and fears were
lost in the night,
and the night was long,
four hundred years-plus long.

Traces of cold night
flow like the Nile
in my veins,
for the journey was not
in vain.

Through resilient eyes
I speak words of the
night travelers unable to
utter sounds of freedom.

I am a seed
planted on that night,

and the night was long
four hundred years plus-long.

Dawn greets me kindly today,
brilliant sun in my eyes.
I am the destination.
With pride I speak for
the unspoken.

Good morning, America
the journey has arrived.

Airport in Teguc.

You stood behind the gate,
skin and hair dyed by a different
sun. You blended with the natives.
Only when you smiled
and looked through me
with those talking eyes
did I know it was you,
picking me up
from the airport
in Teguc.

Miss America *(If it were up to me)*

"A native of Cleveland,
straight off Superior Ave.,
Imani is five six,
better known to family
and friends as "Cornbread"
because she's thick like that.
She enjoys revolutionary work
on a grass roots level, volunteering
at her local community center
helping young kids read better.
Her bronze complexion and high
cheek bones are
accented today by her
"mud cloth" head wrap.
She enjoys listening to
Miles Davis and Sonny Rollins
and stays in shape by teaching
African dance to young kids on her block.
Imani studies the origins
of African American literature at
Black University. It is with great
pleasure I introduce the NEW
Miss America." (If it were up to me)

His Love

His love sits,
collecting interest
like old money,
ricochetting from the depths
of nothing.

His love is frozen,
waiting to be thawed by
his own need to be touched.

His love hurts,
stabbing at the core of
your vulnerability,
knowing that your solace is him.

Amiably you remain,
waiting for the pendulum of his
love to swing your way.

But like his love,
your soul waits, reserved,
collecting interest like old money.

Its pain resonating through your eyes.
One day someone will see,
and fall in love.

All My Sisters

Gold,
bronze,
chocolate,
mocha, yellow,
tan,
mahogany,
beige,
ebony, copper,
sunshine, evening,
night,
charcoal,
lemon,. peach,
caramel, cinnamon,
nutmeg,
honey, khaki,
toffee.
Damn, all my sisters!

Just Like Mama

Just like Mama, you want to
know everywhere I go,
not being nosey but it
comforts you to know.
Frowning if I come in late at
night, yet relieved when I make
it home all right.
Just like Mama

Making sure only the best for me,
especially when life
has gotten the best of me.
Just like Mama.

I feel your wrath when I'm wrong,
but you still love me,
it never lasts for long.
There when I need you most,
even at breakfast spreading
butter on my toast.
Just like Mama.

The woman I wish I could marry,
inside your womb my child you'd carry.
You're the woman that I love,
you make me happy,
just like Mama.

In a Daze

As I sit here gazed at the beauty
of your face dazed, half crazed,
amazed at your ways
asking myself, "Is this just a phase?"
My passion for you ablazed,
burning endlessly for days. The grace
of your walk plays with my eyes
hidden behind shades, raised
at the sight of your soft, silky legs,
appearing to be glazed from
the sun's natural rays.
I'm found lost in your display,
way off in a daze.

*BROTHERS GONNA
WORK IT OUT*

10/16/95
(The Million Man March)

From the brisk darkness of morning
they came, ambassadors of the
downtrodden, congressmen
of under-represented hoods.
A rising sun brought warmth to greetings,
revealing the dreams of ancestors,
the silent cries of sisters,
and the necessity of tomorrow;
Black men embraced,
marveling at themselves,
void of exaggerated maleness,
detached from false pride.
Poured of water, not beer,
represented "the brothers who ain't here."
No "pick-up" games began
and "Cops" ran reruns, for its stars
had another place to be
on 10/16/95.

Brothers

Different shapes, various hues
an array of styles and vocabularies used
Harvard or Hard Knocks
suburban streets or city blocks

Diverse as the clothes we wear
the songs we sing
the women we choose
the talents we bring

Black-berry, brown sugar, or high yellow
laid-back, high strung, or just mellow
six-seven or five-eight
on time or always late

Different as the flowers hit by the sun
yet still public enemy number one
afros or waves, Wall Street or not
a negative image is what we've got

Dead serious or full of fun
trigger-happy or scared of guns
King's English or Ghetto Slang
too many brothers constitute a gang

smiles come our way
when we dance and clown
but quickly turn to frowns
when pants hang down

Loving father or dead-beat-dad
as pleasant as the sun or always mad
differences don't matter
when it's all said and done
because a brother is a brother,
public enemy number one

Soldia

I'm a soldia' because I battle each day with
racists with smiling faces, fearful of what I
bring to their work places. Armed with fake
smiles and salutations delivered with Amos
and Andy-like exaggerations. I run for cover
to reload, because as I'm told, "Keep smilin'
chile!" All the while, disrupting my smooth,
cool, soul-brother-number-one style. My
cheeks get tired, but if I'm not happy I'm
fired. I'm a soldia'.

My fatigues aren't green, they're not that
type, rather they're khakis and oxfords with
ties tied tight. I watch other brothers with
chagrin as they scramble to blend in with
their walk, their talk and the cliques they
move in. They cringe at Ebonics but after
work confide in gin and tonics to drown
their shame, they give in and call it a game.
Not me, I'm a soldia'.

Some brothers bite their tongues on
important issues, then run for tissues to dry
their eyes because they sell-out to lies and
wear silly disguises.

They scurry around with their heads to the ground, at least when a soldia' comes around. But I ain't mad at them, it's "all good", I mean, it's "cool," damn, can't use those words, they're inappropriate too. I can't fake it, I won't make it, if it's "like that" then take it and keep it, my life is truth so I seek it. I'm a soldia' by day, resting at night, I try to play but instead I fight.

My own people can't stand me, the boss doesn't understand me I walk off-beat, heart pumping blood from urban streets, places they dare to dwell, they say it's worst than hell, I am happy, they just can't tell. And I'm not a chameleon, I resist the change, to me it's a war, don't like those games. I'm a soldia'

Despite my degrees and intellect, I'm handcuffed by fears, subject to disrespect, always a suspect, it's got me wanting to flex and wring necks, the hell with a check!...but ain't that what they expect? Instead I search

for words I learned in their class to tell them
politely and intellectually to kiss my ass.
Built to endure pain and stress, there's no
room for timidness, I release things from my
chest. Sometimes I wish I could let things
be, but the creator created this warrior in
me. Someone has to deal with the ones who
bought and sold ya', I guess that's me, since
I'm a soldia'

I used to laugh at brothers in their Brooks
Brothers suits, accusing them of selling-out
for loot. But now when I see them with ties
around their necks, I "dap" them up to show
love and respect. I refuse to judge by what I
see, they could be be a soldia' just like me.

At home at night I sigh deep and sleep,
praying for inner-peace, but I'm awaken by
the sound of my people fighting in the
streets. They need to suit up and come fight
with me, but we still suffer from that slave
mentality. It's too much for some to carry
on their shoulders, so give it to me like I
told ya', because I'm a soldia', I'm a soldia.

Still Here
(For the ancestors)

Openings in torture "castles"
framed the vast blue unknown.
Waves that once sent forth
life-sustaining tides were
now pathways to hell without fire.
But they're still here.

Blue-black skin bore visible scars of
pierced flesh, but the spirit remained
unscathed.
Nothing could tie up their will to exist.

Nature in a new world
became tools of oppression
providing height and hook for
white-tied nooses.
Their blackness became
the purpose for hate, the grounds
for injustice.
But they're still here.

You see,
they planted seeds,

knowing that their life lived
in things to come,
and I came,
and they're still here.

Things Done Changed

What's up player?
I see you walk around
With your face all frowned
Pants hanging down,
Too cool for words.
I just got one question
as you stroll the boulevard
Since when did you become
so tough and hard?
Don't get me wrong, I know you ain't soft
But your gun-totin' and drug sellin'
got me at a loss
With your new found toughness
most can't tell
But you can't fool me, I know you too well
I understand the "game"
When handling your business
things do change
But why front on me?
We've been boys for years
Don't you remember crying together,
then laughing at our tears?
I thought maybe we just grew apart
But I know what's in your heart

We were raised the same,
our moms were tight
Sitting on the porch
watching us play at night
I ain't mad at cha' I know the deal
I just don't understand when you tell *me* to
"keep it real". I thought I was,
I remember our pact
Grow up and get paid and always comeback
To Show the youth what life is about
Love and family, not money and clout
So keep doing your thing I understand
That the game sometimes changes the man
It's just sad about your particular case
Because you're strong and
could uplift our race
I just wanted to holler at you
since I saw you today
Tell your mom and 'em I said hey
Stop by sometimes
when making your rounds
Maybe we can chill like old times
...if no one is around

Guess What

My daddy got an uncle
named Eddie and
guess what,
he's my uncle too

He always got stories
to tell and tells them to
anyone who listens
and he tells them to people
who don't want to listen too,
and guess what

Uncle Eddie knows a lot about
a lot of stuff and he makes
people laugh when he tells them
stuff and guess what

Sometimes he doesn't make sense
at first when he talks but
somehow you understand
at the end and guess what

I used to run the other way when
Uncle Eddie came around but then

I stopped running because his stories
are funny and guess what

I learn a lot about my family
and about life
from his stories and guess what

Uncle Eddie always says
"guess what" just to
keep you listening until
he's done.

The Hood in Me

Some say it's the hood in me
That blankets the good in me
And I need to leave it behind
But love of the hood runs deep within
And gives me a humbled state of mind
To castrate the hood in me, to sever ties,
Is to uproot a tree or ground
A bird born for the skies
The hood is my foundation
Allowing me to face a nation
That says it's impossible to overcome obstacles
Prevalent in the hood, but I'm here
And it's "all good"
I can "chill" on Wall Street" looking
"fly" on my way, all with the hood
beneath me, because it's a new day.

A Gathering of Old Men

Until today they were just old men.
Nameless figures in the window of Sam's
five and dime. A red light at 26th
and Madison force me to sit this morning.

Intriguing they are, dusty hats, brown,
flaky cigars dangling loosely from their
lips. Through the smoke I see their eyes,
deep and clear. Wrinkled,
mahogany hands that have long since retired
balance wooden canes by their seats.
White beards resembling cotton
line their handsome, sunken faces.
Morning schoolers enter their world,
seeking treats or safety from dangerous
streets. But the men don't move- statues
posing for onlookers eager
to know their purpose. Their
silence comforting one another.

Shrieking horns interrupt my gaze
as I stare between scratches
in the plastic window at a ceremonial
gathering of old men, nothing more.

Blue Lights

Each swing of blue light
slices the night exposing the
guts of a wounded city,
revealing the twisted brows
of Black men holding back
fiery tongues and shaking hands
as operators of the blue lights
determine their fate.

Black boots clank the concrete
and blue lights cast shadows
of Caprice Classics and night
sticks swinging from eager arms.

We're all classified as thugs
in this cold war on drugs
posing for mug shots,
spreading eagle on city blocks,
placed in cells that lock tight.
Yell out, call to be bailed out
or else find a spot and spend the night.

Blue lights stretch far
into the night, waving the air

like Old Glory, shining
light on a retold story that
keeps coming back.
It's scary to see blue lights
at night when driving while black.

Upon His Knee

He was always prepared with
wisdom-filled phrases for each
dilemma I faced. No rite-of-passage
initiation too complex for his wise soul
blessed with the gift of wound-healing gab.
Young days too many in number
I fell victim to idle time
and his presence. Shared time
and space to him was God-granted
opportunity to water his seed hungry for
growth. In transparent eyes he saw to my
soul's disarray. Left-field analogies rolled
from his tongue like waterfalls cleansing
debris-filled rocks below.
His truths backed up by his
own "manchild in the promised land"
experiences. In the twinkling of my
listening eyes, his epilogue travels 360
degrees, slapping the obvious in my youthful
face. I smile at his performance and
dismount from his knee. And now, well
beyond the threshold of manhood,
I understand.

The Subway Home

My matching luggage,
new glasses, and this Alice Walker
book in my hand
make me vulnerable, suspect.

They don't know how to take me,
these four dudes sitting across from me.
"He looks like one of us,"
their eyes say, but no lips dare speak it.
But missing from my demeanor is
that edge I once had,
that "I don't care about anything
or anybody-look" I used to have.

I struggle to muster up hostility
on my face, just enough to get
me to Windemere Station, but I don't
have it anymore, at least not *that* kind.
They're still staring.

I want to gaze out the window
to see my old city zip by, but
I refrain- can't seem like
a naive tourist.

In a flash my face frowns
and I grit my teeth. Now I'm mad.
Mad at my paranoia, angry
at what we have become. Distant
brothers always trying to figure
each other out.

I am Your Teacher

Good morning. Glad you made it.
You could have stayed away and
been justified, but you came.
Angry at times, yet the first
in line you stand.
I am your teacher.

I came early today myself,
to organize my mental shelf, so I can
be free to be what you need
me to be- brother, father, friend.
I am your teacher.

I want you to love your hood
but understand it's not "all good,"
yet worthy of your respect nevertheless.
I am your teacher.

I often gaze, watching you work,
avoiding conflict with others
and I catch glimpses of my young self,
too eager and mad, but grateful still

for the teachers I had.
And today, you look to me.
I am your teacher.

I turn to the mirror behind my
desk, staring in the face of that once
fearful child scared of success.
I draw strength from your eyes that
speak volumes. With expectations
of excellence from us both,
I begin my day.
I am your teacher.

Strapped

With one shrieking moan he
was gone, just like that. My boy died
too soon because he wasn't strapped.
He traveled unarmed to prove he was bold
unaware that his story would soon be told.
His killer is ruthless, waiting for young men
to slip, just like my boy, thought he
wouldn't be hit. We had each other's backs,
it was always like that, since boyhood days
and school yard scraps. I try to catch
this killer but he eludes all traps. Like
snow in the south and a clear bright moon,
my boy wasn't strapped so he died too soon.
I got revenge on my mind, the hell with a
truce, an eye for an eye, a tooth for a tooth.
Being strapped is my only defense
against this heartless nemesis.
I miss my friend and there's one thing I know,
I must be strapped or be the next one to go.
My boy taught me a damn good lesson,
stay strapped always, no second guessing
...with a condom.

Pass it On

Like a game of "it"
pass it on, before it's too late
and the moment is gone.
It doesn't help to keep it close,
when young eyes show they
need it the most.
Pass it on.

It does no good to keep it in,
a cardinal sin, considering where
our people have been. Talk of
times, pleasant and sad, when our
people held true and loved what they had.
Pass it on.

Speak of yesterday,
block parties and village times,
when through the rain,
the sun shined bright. Tell the how
Harriet led us to freedom at night.
Pass it On.

Share the history that schools leave out
so our children will know what their
past is about. Don't scorn our
kids and say they're wrong,
if you didn't take the time to
Pass it On.

County Blues

I pose for this picture
to be seen by eyes I have yet to see.
In the background is my pastime,
illustrations of life outside the county
recalled from a memory that struggles to
remember such days.
From this photo he will never
know the smell of prison air or the piercing
sound of nighttime here. He won't
know my style because those posing
by my side look just like me,
dressed in these county blues.
Our identities unclear because the
numbers on our shirt, also our names,
are too small to see.
He won't know that his smile
is like mine; in this photo I frown.
Smiles here are invitations to whatever.
My pose is untrue, hiding hands behind
my back, shielding my weapons,
battered and scarred from
struggles to exist. In this photographic
attempt at rasing my son I cry,
inside of course.

Index of poems by first lines

Index of poem first lines

To order additional copies of

Coco Ways

or

To schedule author readings or
book signings, contact:

AYA Publishing

5007 C Victory Blvd.

Suite # 191

Yorktown, Virginia 23693

ayabooks@aol.com